Colorful World of Animals

Betta Fish

by Cecilia Pinto McCarthy

Consulting Editor: Gail Saunders-Smith, PhD

Consultant: Brooke Weinstein, Biologist II
Steinhart Aquarium
California Academy of Sciences

CAPSTONE PRESS
a capstone imprint

Pebble Plus is published by Capstone Press,
151 Good Counsel Drive, P.O. Box 669, Mankato, Minnesota 56002.
www.capstonepub.com

Books published by Capstone Press are manufactured with paper containing at least 10 percent post-consumer waste.

Library of Congress Cataloging-in-Publication Data
McCarthy, Cecilia Pinto.
  Betta fish / by Cecilia Pinto McCarthy.
    p. cm.—(Pebble plus. Colorful world of animals)
  Includes bibliographical references and index.
  Summary: "Simple text and full-color photos explain the habitat, range, life cycle, and behavior of betta fish while emphasizing their bright colors"—Provided by publisher.
  ISBN 978-1-4296-6051-8 (library binding)
  1. Betta—Juvenile literature. I. Title.
  QL638.B347M33 2012
  597'.7—dc22   2011000267

Editorial Credits
Katy Kudela, editor; Lori Bye, designer; Svetlana Zhurkin, media researcher; Laura Manthe, production specialist

Photo Credits
Dreamstime/Jeremy Wee, 16–17
iStockphoto/Cristian Baitg, 1
Minden Pictures/Foto Natura/Wil Meinderts, cover, 4–5; Fumitoshi Mori, 19
Nature Picture Library/Jane Burton, 8–9
Oliver Lucanus, 7
Photolibrary/Peter Arnold/Max Gibbs, 11
Shutterstock/mnoor, 20–21; MountainHardcore, 12–13, 15

Note to Parents and Teachers

The Colorful World of Animals series supports national science standards related to life science. This book describes and illustrates betta fish. The images support early readers in understanding the text. The repetition of words and phrases helps early readers learn new words. This book also introduces early readers to subject-specific vocabulary words, which are defined in the Glossary section. Early readers may need assistance to read some words and to use the Table of Contents, Glossary, Read More, Internet Sites, and Index sections of the book.

Printed in the United States of America in North Mankato, Minnesota.
032011
006110CGF11

Table of Contents

Author's Note

There are more than 65 species of fish known as betta (BEHT-uh). This book describes *Betta splendens,* commonly known as Siamese fighting fish.

Rainbow Fish

Swish! A brightly colored
betta swirls its long fins.
Bettas have many
colors and patterns.

Found in Asia, wild bettas
are freshwater fish with duller
colors. They live in rice paddies
and marshes. Colorful pet bettas
were bred from wild bettas.

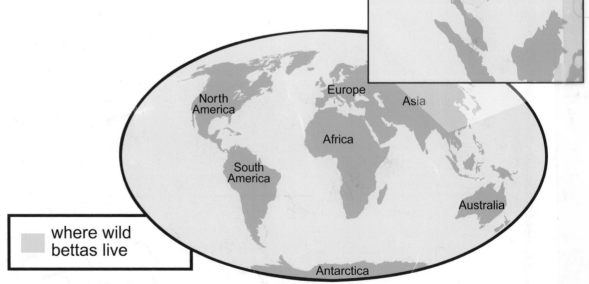

where wild
bettas live

North
America

Europe

Asia

Africa

South
America

Australia

Antarctica

Betta Bodies

Bettas grow up to 3 inches
(7.6 centimeters) long. Males
have longer fins than females.
Females are not as colorful
or as large as male bettas.

Bettas can live in shallow water.

Like most fish, they use gills

to breathe underwater.

Unlike most fish, they also gulp

air from the water's surface.

gill

Bettas have strong mouths.
In the wild, they snatch
insects and worms drifting
on the water. Pet bettas eat
fish pellets and flakes.

Fighting Fish

Bettas are called "fighting fish" because males fight each other. Males will even fight their own reflections. They do not like to share their space.

When male bettas fight,

they try to look scary.

They stretch their fins.

They puff out their gill covers.

Their colors get brighter too.

Hatching and Growing

Male bettas build bubble nests.

Females lay hundreds of eggs.

Males catch eggs with their

mouths. They blow the eggs

into the floating nest.

Betta fry hatch in a day.

Males guard the small fry.

After two to three days,

the fry can live on their own.

Bettas live up to five years.

fry

21

Glossary

bred—to produce an animal with certain features

dull—not bright

fin—a body part that fish use to swim and steer in water

fry—baby fish

gill cover—a fold of skin that protects a fish's gill; fish breathe with their gills

hatch—to break out of an egg

marsh—an area of wet, low land

paddy—a wet field where rice is grown

pattern—a repeating order of colors or shapes

pellet—a small, hard ball of food

reflection—an image made by or as if made by a mirror

shallow—not deep

Read More

Richardson, Adele. *Caring for Your Fish.* Positively Pets. Mankato, Minn.: Capstone Press, 2007.

Slade, Suzanne. *Fish: Finned and Gilled Animals.* Amazing Science: Animal Classification. Minneapolis: Picture Window Books, 2010.

Internet Sites

FactHound offers a safe, fun way to find Internet sites related to this book. All of the sites on FactHound have been researched by our staff.

Here's all you do:

Visit *www.facthound.com*

Type in this code: 9781429660518

Check out projects, games and lots more at
www.capstonekids.com

Index

Word Count: 218
Grade: 1
Early-Intervention Level: 15